Fundamentals Paper F6
Taxation FA 2011

First edition April 2007
Sixth edition January 2012

ISBN 9781 4453 8067 4 (previous ISBN 9780 7517 9419 9)

e ISBN 9781 4453 7601 1

British Library Cataloguing-in-Publication Data

A catalogue record for this book is available from the British Library
Published by

BPP Learning Media Ltd, BPP House, Aldine Place, London W12 8AA

www.bpp.com/learningmedia

Printed in the United Kingdom

Your learning materials, published by BPP Learning Media Ltd,
are printed on paper sourced from sustainable, managed forests.

Welcome to BPP Learning Media's ACCA **Passcards** for **Fundamentals Paper F6 Taxation (UK).**

- They **save you time**. Important topics are summarised for you.

- They incorporate **diagrams** to kick start your memory.

- They follow the overall **structure** of the BPP Learning Media Study Texts, but BPP Learning Media's ACCA **Passcards** are not just a condensed book. Each card has been separately designed for clear presentation. Topics are self contained and can be grasped visually.

- ACCA **Passcards** are still **just the right size** for pockets, briefcases and bags.

- ACCA **Passcards focus on the exam** you will be facing.

Run through the complete set of **Passcards** as often as you can during your final revision period. The day before the exam, try to go through the **Passcards** again! You will then be well on your way to passing your exams.

Good luck!

		Page			**Page**

Contents

Notes

1: Introduction to the UK tax system

Topic List

The overall function and purpose of taxation in a modern economy

Different types of taxes

Principal sources of revenue law and practice

Tax avoidance and tax evasion

This chapter contains background knowledge which underpins the whole of your later studies of taxation.

Economic factors

Taxation represents a withdrawal from the UK economy. Tax policies can be used to encourage and discourage certain types of activity.

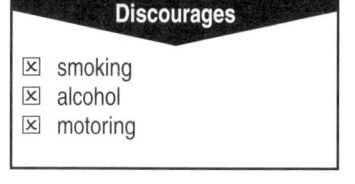

Encourages

- ☑ saving
- ☑ charitable donations
- ☑ entrepreneurs
- ☑ investment in plant and machinery

Discourages

- ☒ smoking
- ☒ alcohol
- ☒ motoring

Social factors

Tax policies can be used to redistribute wealth

- Direct taxes – tax only those who have these resources
- Indirect taxes – discourage spending
- Progressive taxes – target those who can afford to pay

Environmental factors

Taxes may be levied for environmental reasons

- Climate change levy
- Landfil tax

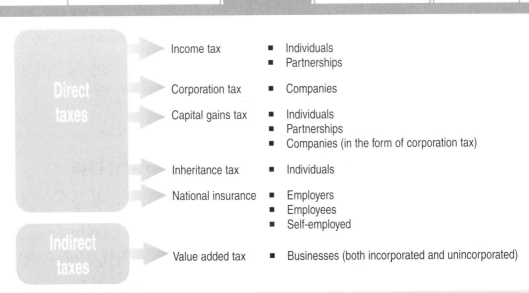

Direct taxes

Income tax
- Individuals
- Partnerships

Corporation tax
- Companies

Capital gains tax
- Individuals
- Partnerships
- Companies (in the form of corporation tax)

Inheritance tax
- Individuals

National insurance
- Employers
- Employees
- Self-employed

Indirect taxes

Value added tax
- Businesses (both incorporated and unincorporated)

Structure of the UK Tax system

Treasury

HM Revenue and Customs

- Officers of Revenue and Customs
- Receivables management officers
- Revenue and Customs Prosecutions Office

Appeals heard by

- First Tier Tribunal (most cases)
- Upper Tribunal (complex cases)

Sources of revenue law and practice

Law

Statute
Statutory instrument

Practice

Statements of practice
Extra-statutory concessions
Explanatory leaflets
Business economic notes
Revenue and Customs Brief
Internal Guidance (HMRC manuals)
Working Together

Tax evasion

Tax evasion consists of seeking to mislead HMRC by either:

- Suppressing information, or

- Providing deliberately false information.

Illegal

Tax avoidance

Tax avoidance includes any legal method of reducing your tax burden, eg

- Using tax shelters, or

- Participating in schemes designed to minimise tax.

Legal

Concerns whether client is honest with HMRC

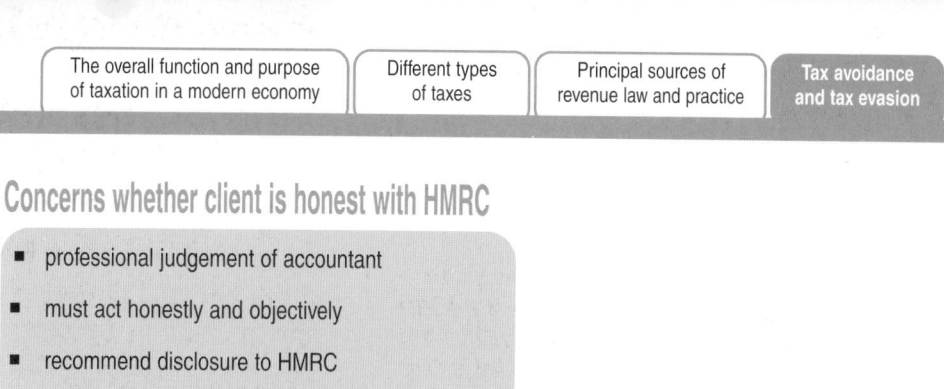

- professional judgement of accountant

- must act honestly and objectively

- recommend disclosure to HMRC

- if no disclosure, cease to act ●━━━━━━━━━● inform HMRC but not details of why

- make money laundering report

avoid 'tipping-off' the client

2: The computation of taxable income and the income tax liability

The computation of income tax is a key exam topic. This chapter deals with the income tax computation which draws together all of the taxpayer's income. The following chapters will cover the rules for computing taxable income from each different source.

An individual who is resident in the UK is taxable on his worldwide income.

Resident

An individual is resident in the UK if he:

- Is present in the UK for 183 days or more, or
- Makes visits to the UK averaging 91 days per year or more over four consecutive years.

Net income

Total income minus deductible interest and trade losses.

Adjusted net income

Net income less grossed up gift aid/personal pension contributions.

Aggregation of income

A basic principle of income tax is the **aggregation of income.** All of an individual's income for a tax year is added up in a personal tax computation as **total income.**

Taxable income

Net income minus personal allowance.

Tax liability

The amount of tax charged on income.

Tax payable

The balance of the tax liability still to be paid.

Personal allowance

Individual aged < 65
£7,475 for 2011/12

Individual aged ⩾ 65
£9,940 age 65-74 for 2011/12
£10,090 age 75+ for 2011/12

Restrict if adjusted net income > £100,000 by £1 for each £2 excess (nil if ⩾ £114,950).

Restrict if adjusted net income > £24,000 by £1 for each £2 excess to minimum £7,475 (unless income > £100,000, then restrict as for standard allowance)

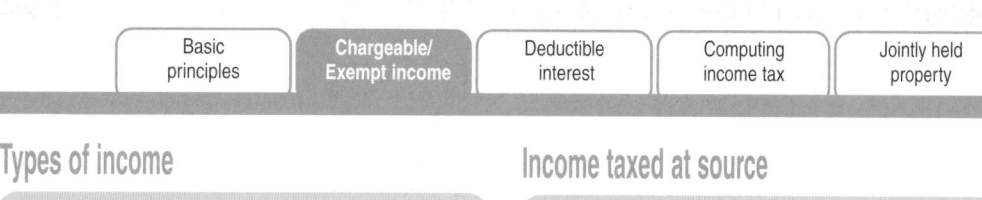

Types of income

The main types of income for individuals are:

- Profits of trades, professions and vocations
- Income from employment and pensions
- Property income
- Savings and investment income, including interest and dividends

Exempt income

Leave exempt income out of personal tax computations.

- Premium bond prizes
- Income from Individual Savings Accounts (ISAs)
- Returns on National Savings Certificates

Income taxed at source

Many sorts of investment income are taxed at source: for every £100 of income, the individual only receives £80 of interest or £90 of dividends from UK companies. The taxable income is both cases is £100, but credit is given for the tax suffered.

This applies to bank and building society interest.

Tax credits on dividends can be offset to reduce a tax bill but are never repaid to a taxpayer. Tax credits on other taxed income can be repaid.

Deductible interest

Interest paid on a particular type of loan is deducted from total income to compute net income.

- For purchase of an interest in a partnership, or
- For purchase of plant and machinery for partnership (purchase must be by partner), or
- For purchase of plant and machinery for use in employment (purchase must be by employee)

2: The computation of taxable income and the income tax liability

Computing income tax

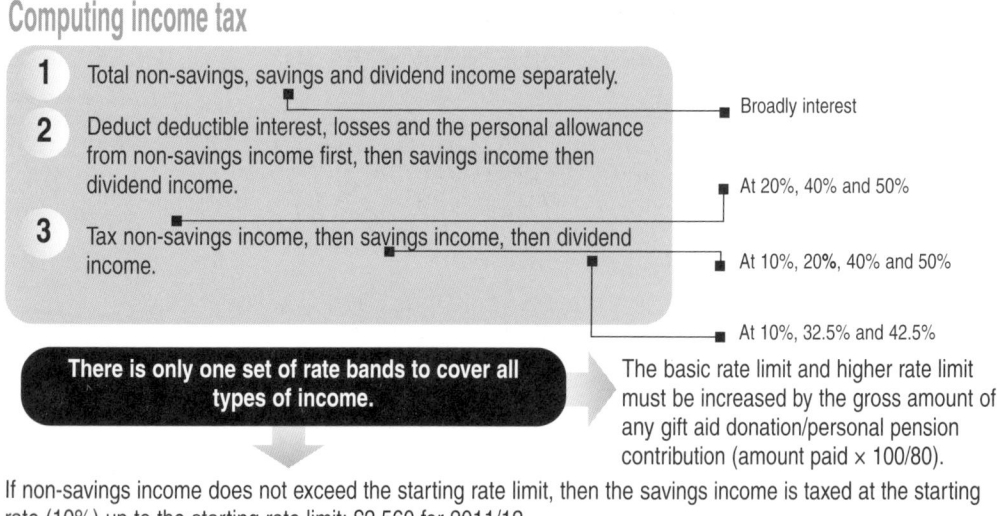

1 Total non-savings, savings and dividend income separately.

■ Broadly interest

2 Deduct deductible interest, losses and the personal allowance from non-savings income first, then savings income then dividend income.

■ At 20%, 40% and 50%

3 Tax non-savings income, then savings income, then dividend income.

■ At 10%, 20%, 40% and 50%

■ At 10%, 32.5% and 42.5%

There is only one set of rate bands to cover all types of income.

The basic rate limit and higher rate limit must be increased by the gross amount of any gift aid donation/personal pension contribution (amount paid × 100/80).

If non-savings income does not exceed the starting rate limit, then the savings income is taxed at the starting rate (10%) up to the starting rate limit: £2,560 for 2011/12.

Jointly held property

Spouses and civil partners often hold property jointly, sometimes in unequal proportions.

For tax purposes treat the income received from such property as shared equally.

If the actual interests in the property are unequal, spouses/civil partners can declare this to HMRC and income is then shared in actual proportions.

Notes

3: Employment income

Topic List

Employment and self-employment

Basis of assessment

Allowable deductions

Although this exam is mainly computational you may be asked to describe the difference between employment and self-employment.

You also need to be aware of the final two topics in this chapter: when employment income is assessed and the deductions that you may be able to make in computing the amount of assessable employment income.

Employed or self-employed

An employee works under a contract of service and a self-employed person under a contract for services.

Whether a contract is a contract of service or a contract for services will depend on a number of factors.

Factors

- The degree of control exercised over the person doing the work
- Whether he must accept further work
- Whether the other party must provide further work
- Whether he provides his own equipment
- Whether entitled to benefits eg pension
- Whether he hires his own helpers
- What degree of financial risk he takes
- What degree of responsibility for investment and management he has
- Whether he can profit from sound management
- Whether he can work when he chooses
- The wording used in any agreement between parties

Employment income

Employees/directors are taxed on income from the employment:

- Cash earnings
- Benefits

Earnings are taxed in the year in which they are received.

The general definition of the date of receipt is the earlier of:

- The time payment is made
- The time entitlement to payment arises

Directors are deemed to receive earnings on the earliest of the following:

- The time given by the general rule
- The time the amount is credited in the company's accounting records
- The end of the company's period of account (if the amount has been determined by then)
- When the amount is determined (if after the end of the company's period of account)

Employment and
self-employment

Basis
of assessment

Allowable
deductions

The general rule is that expenses can only be deducted from earnings if they are incurred wholly, exclusively and necessarily in performing the duties of the employment.

- The strictness of this test has been emphasised in many cases

Expenses specifically deductible against earnings:

1 **Insurance** premiums to cover directors' and employees' liabilities (and payments to meet those liabilities)

2 **Subscriptions** to relevant professional bodies

3 **Qualifying travel expenses** – costs the employee incurs travelling in the performance of his duties or/and travelling to or from a place attended in the performance of duties

4 **Contributions** (within limits) to a registered occupational pension scheme

5 **Payments to charity** under a payroll deduction scheme

- Normal commuting does not qualify
- Relief is available for expenses incurred by an employee working at a temporary location on a secondment of 24 months or less
- If a mileage allowance is paid relief is available for any shortfall of allowance actually paid over statutory mileage allowance

Exam focus

If you have to decide whether an expense is deductible, put yourself in HMRC's position and try to find an argument against deducting it. If you can find a specific argument, the expense is probably not deductible.

4: Taxable and exempt benefits. The PAYE system

Benefits are often examined so it is vital that you are able to calculate the taxable value of benefits provided to employees. You also need to be aware of the benefits that are exempt from tax.

The deduction of tax from employment income through the PAYE system is less frequently examined, but it is still important.

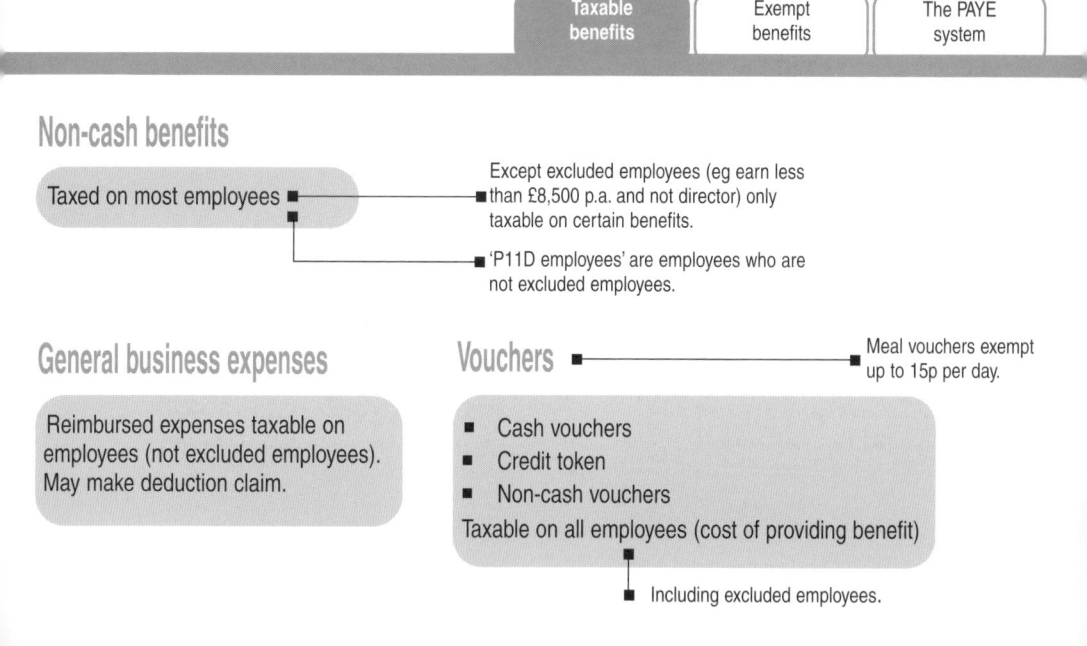

Non-cash benefits

Taxed on most employees

Except excluded employees (eg earn less than £8,500 p.a. and not director) only taxable on certain benefits.

'P11D employees' are employees who are not excluded employees.

General business expenses

Reimbursed expenses taxable on employees (not excluded employees). May make deduction claim.

Vouchers

Meal vouchers exempt up to 15p per day.

- Cash vouchers
- Credit token
- Non-cash vouchers

Taxable on all employees (cost of providing benefit)

Including excluded employees.

Accommodation

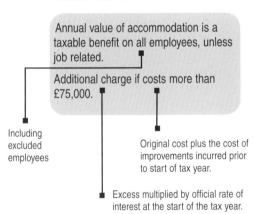

Annual value of accommodation is a taxable benefit on all employees, unless job related.

Additional charge if costs more than £75,000.

Including excluded employees

Original cost plus the cost of improvements incurred prior to start of tax year.

Excess multiplied by official rate of interest at the start of the tax year.

Living expenses

Living expenses connected with accommodation (eg gas bills) are taxable on P11D employees only. However, if the accommodation is job-related, the maximum amount taxable is 10% of net earnings.

Vans

£3,000 charge if available for private use (not home/work commuting).

£550 charge for private fuel.

Loans

1. Loans of over £5,000 give rise to taxable benefits equal to the difference between the actual interest and interest at the official rate.

2. A write-off of a loan gives rise to a taxable benefit equal to the amount written off.

Only taxed on P11D employees

Cars

Annual taxable benefit for the private use of a car is (price of car – capital contributions) × %.

- Cars emitting 75g/km or less = 5%
- Cars emitting CO_2 between 76–120g/km = 10%.
- Cars emitting between 121–125g/km = 15%. Percentage increases by 1% for each 5g/km (rounded down) up to 35%.
- Percentage increased by 3% for diesel engined cars (not above max 35%).
- Benefit scaled down on a time basis, if car not available all year. Benefit then reduced by any contribution by employee for private use.
- Fuel for private use is charged as percentage of base figure (£18,800, 2011/12). Same percentage as car benefit. No reduction for partial reimbursement by the employee.

Private use of asset

In general, if an asset is made available for private use, the annual taxable benefit is 20% of the market value when the asset was first provided, less any employee contribution.

If the asset is subsequently given to the employee the taxable benefit is the higher of:

- (i) Original MV less amounts already taxed
- (ii) Market value at date of gift less any employee contribution.

■ Not used if asset is bicycle

Other benefits

- Taxable value of other benefits charged on employees other than excluded employees
- Excluded employees taxed only on secondhand value as cash earnings

Cost of provision of benefit less any amount made good by employee

4: Taxable and exempt benefits. The PAYE system

Exempt benefits

Loans of up to £5,000

Meal vouchers of up to 15p per day

Entertainment and gifts provided by a third party for an employee by reason of his employment
- The cost of gifts from any one source must not exceed £250 per tax year

Long service awards of up to £50 per year of service
- The award must be a non-cash award and the employee must have worked at least 20 years

Job related accommodation

Workplace nurseries

Other childcare provided by employer
- Limited to £55/£28/£22 per week for basic/higher/additional rate employee

Recreational/sporting facilities available to employees generally

Works buses and mini-buses
- A minibus must have a seating capacity of 9 or more. A works bus must have a seating capacity of 12 or more

Bicycles provided for cycling to work

Parking places at or near work

| Taxable benefits | Exempt benefits | The PAYE system |

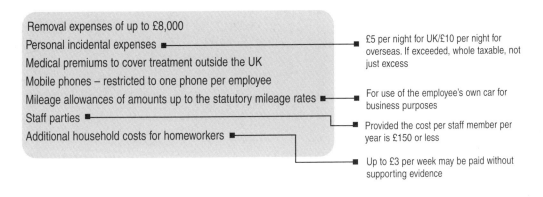

Removal expenses of up to £8,000

Personal incidental expenses ■————————————— £5 per night for UK/£10 per night for overseas. If exceeded, whole taxable, not just excess

Medical premiums to cover treatment outside the UK

Mobile phones – restricted to one phone per employee

Mileage allowances of amounts up to the statutory mileage rates ■———— ■ For use of the employee's own car for business purposes

Staff parties ■——————————————

■ Provided the cost per staff member per year is £150 or less

Additional household costs for homeworkers ■————————

■ Up to £3 per week may be paid without supporting evidence

4: Taxable and exempt benefits. The PAYE system

The PAYE system collects tax from employees each payday, with the intention that over a tax year, the correct total of tax due will be collected.

Routine each payday

- Add the gross pay to the running total of gross pay for the tax year
- Use the employee's PAYE code to work out the amount of cumulative gross pay which is tax free
- Compute tax on the balance
- Deduct the tax already paid. The difference is the tax to deduct on this payday

Payment

The employer must pay over the tax deducted up to the 5th of each month by the 19th of the month.

Quarterly payment is allowed if the average monthly total of tax and NICs is less than £1,500

PAYE code numbers

- L: Code with basic personal allowance
- P: Code with age 65-74 allowances
- Y: Code with age 75+ allowance

PAYE settlement agreements

PAYE settlement agreements are arrangements under which employers settle employees' income tax liabilities on certain benefits and expense payments.

Year end returns

Following the year end the employer must submit:
Form P14 } By 19 May
Form P35 }
Form P11D/P9D – by 6 July

5: Pensions

A single regime applies to all pensions, whether occupational or personal.

Pension contributions are a tax efficient way of saving for retirement.

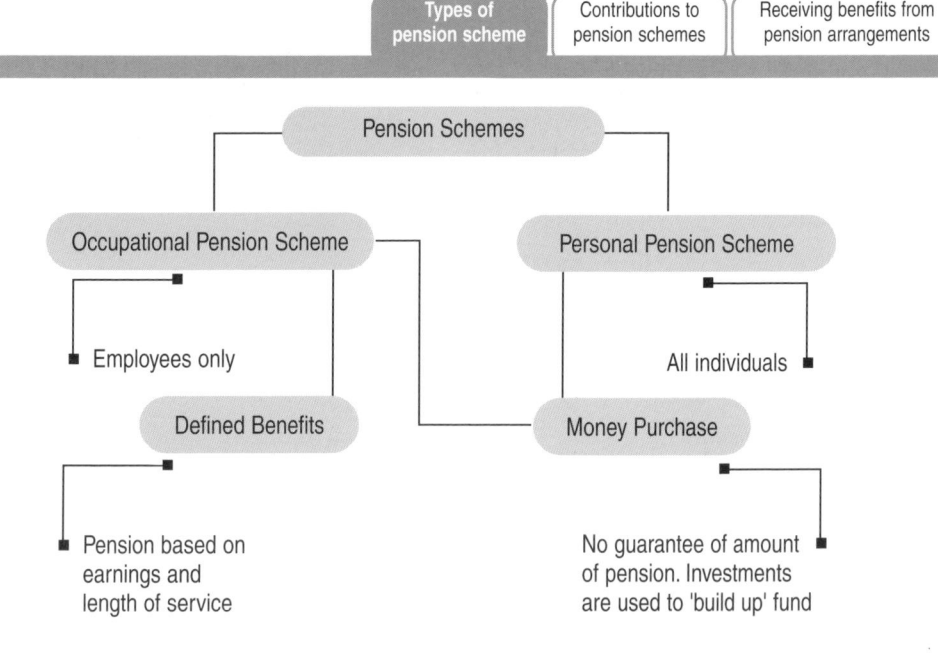

Annual limit

Maximum contribution attracting tax relief is higher of:

- relevant earnings
- £3,600 pa

Lifetime allowance

£1,800,000 is maximum value for pension fund.

Employment income, trading income and furnished holiday lettings income

Annual allowance

- £50,000 for 2011/12
- c/f unused allowance max 3 years
- tax charge on excess – treat as additional non-savings income

Employer contributions:

- Count towards allowances (annual & lifetime)
- Trade deduction for employer
- Tax free benefit for employee
- No NIC for employer or employee

Occupational pension	Personal pension

Occupational pension

Deduct gross employee contributions directly from earnings to find net earnings

Personal pension

- Paid net so automatic 20% tax relief
- Higher rate (and additional rate) taxpayers extend basic rate (and higher rate) limits by gross contributions

deduct from net income to find adjusted net income for PA restriction

This is the same method of giving tax relief as for gift aid donations

```
                    ┌──────────────────┐              ┌──────────────────────────┐
                    │  Pension fund    │─────────────▶│ If fund exceeds lifetime  │
                    │  at retirement   │              │ allowance £1.8m then tax  │
                    └──────────────────┘              │   charge on excess        │
                      │            │                  └──────────────────────────┘
                      ▼            ▼                      │                    │
        ┌──────────────┐   ┌──────────────┐              ▼                    ▼
        │ Tax-free     │   │ Taxable      │      ┌──────────────┐    ┌──────────────┐
        │ lump sum     │   │ annual       │      │ 25% if excess│    │ 55% if excess│
        └──────────────┘   │ pension      │      │ taken as     │    │ taken as     │
                │          │ (usually)    │      │ pension      │    │ lump sum     │
                ▼          └──────────────┘      └──────────────┘    └──────────────┘
        ┌──────────────────┐
        │ Maximum 1/4 of   │
        │ fund             │
        └──────────────────┘
```

Notes

6: Property income

Property income is calculated as if the letting were a business run by the taxpayer.

There are special rules for furnished holiday lettings, and for rooms let in the taxpayer's own home.

Property income is unlikely to be examined in every exam, but when it is examined it could easily form the whole of a 15 mark question.

Property income

Property income covers rent from UK property.

Computation

1. Calculate property income profits on an accruals basis in the same way as you calculate trading profits.

2. Accounts are drawn up as for a sole trader but with a year end of 5 April.

3. Rents and expenses of all properties are pooled to give a single property income figure.

4. If a lease for n years (50 or less) is granted for a premium, the proportion of the premium treated as rent is (premium – (premium × 0.02(n–1))).

Exception
For furnished residential lettings, a 10% wear and tear allowance can be claimed.
Capital allowances are not available.

Exception
Keep a separate pool of profits/losses from letting furnished holiday lettings

Losses

Losses are carried forward against future income from the UK property business.

Furnished holiday lettings

Furnished Holiday Lettings must be

- On a commercial basis
- Available for letting for 140 days in the tax year
- Actually let for 70 days in the tax year
- Not in **longer term occupation** for more than 155 days during the tax year

> ■ Continuous periods of more than 31 days during which the accommodation is in the same occupation

Furnished holiday lettings are treated as a trade for many income tax and CGT purposes

- Rollover relief, entrepreneurs' relief and gift relief are available
- Loss relief – but only c/f against FHL profit
- Capital allowances are available on furniture
- Income is earnings for pension purposes

Rent-a-room scheme

The rent-a-room scheme exempts rent of up to £4,250 a year on rooms in the landlord's main residence.

7: Computing trading income

Topic List

Badges of trade

The adjustment of profits

The 'badges of trade' can be used to determine whether or not an individual is carrying on a trade. If a trade is being carried on, the profits of the trade are taxable as trading income. Otherwise the profit may be taxable as a capital gain.

In this chapter we will look at the badges of trade and at the adjustments needed in the computation of trading income.

This is a key exam topic.

Badges of trade

- The subject matter
- The frequency of transactions
- Similar trading transactions/interests
- The length of ownership
- Organisation as a trade
- Supplementary work and marketing
- A profit motive
- The way in which the asset sold was acquired
- Method of finance
- The taxpayer's intentions

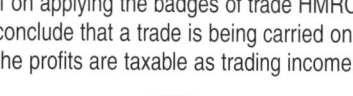

If on applying the badges of trade HMRC conclude that a trade is being carried on, the profits are taxable as trading income.

To arrive at taxable trading profits, the net accounts profit must be adjusted. We look at this in the rest of this chapter.

Certain items of expenditure are not deductible for trading income purposes and so must be added back to the net accounts profit when computing trading profits. Conversely other items are deductible.

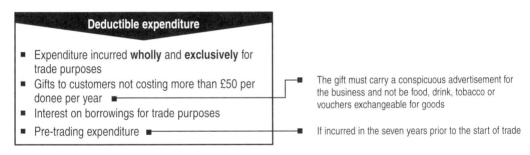

Deductible expenditure

- Expenditure incurred **wholly** and **exclusively** for trade purposes
- Gifts to customers not costing more than £50 per donee per year ■——— ■ The gift must carry a conspicuous advertisement for the business and not be food, drink, tobacco or vouchers exchangeable for goods
- Interest on borrowings for trade purposes
- Pre-trading expenditure ■——— ■ If incurred in the seven years prior to the start of trade

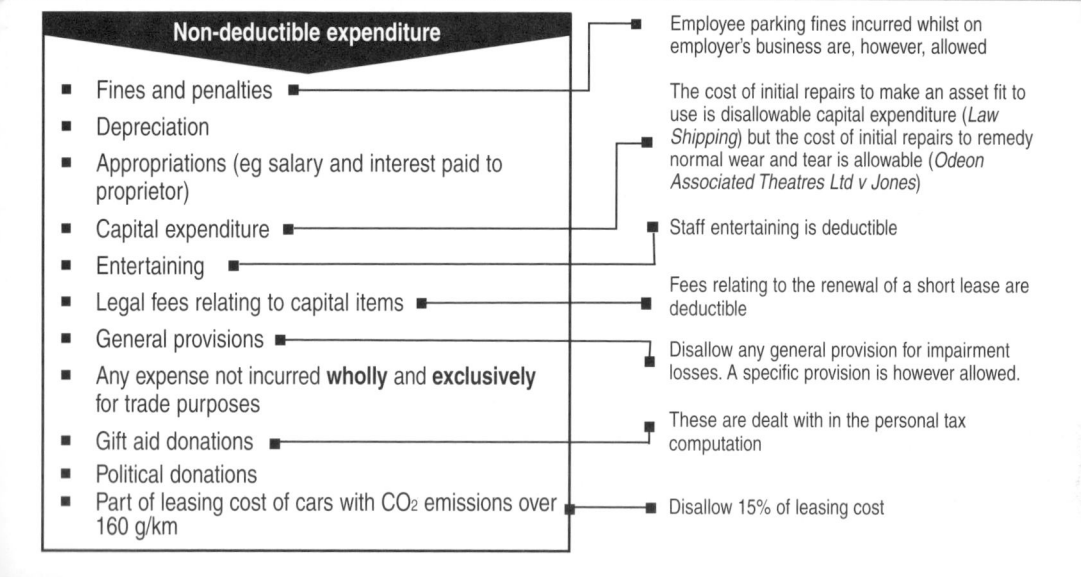

Non-deductible expenditure

- Fines and penalties ■
- Depreciation
- Appropriations (eg salary and interest paid to proprietor)
- Capital expenditure ■
- Entertaining ■
- Legal fees relating to capital items ■
- General provisions ■
- Any expense not incurred **wholly** and **exclusively** for trade purposes
- Gift aid donations ■
- Political donations
- Part of leasing cost of cars with CO$_2$ emissions over 160 g/km

Employee parking fines incurred whilst on employer's business are, however, allowed

The cost of initial repairs to make an asset fit to use is disallowable capital expenditure (*Law Shipping*) but the cost of initial repairs to remedy normal wear and tear is allowable (*Odeon Associated Theatres Ltd v Jones*)

■ Staff entertaining is deductible

■ Fees relating to the renewal of a short lease are deductible

■ Disallow any general provision for impairment losses. A specific provision is however allowed.

These are dealt with in the personal tax computation

■ Disallow 15% of leasing cost

8: Capital allowances

Topic List

Capital allowances are given instead of depreciation, on plant and machinery. They are trading expenses deducted in arriving at taxable trading profits.

Capital allowances are a frequently examined topic.

There are two sources of the rules on what qualifies as plant and is therefore eligible for capital allowances.

Statute

Statutory exclusions

The following items are excluded as plant by statute.

- Buildings and parts of buildings
  - however, utility systems provided to meet the particular requirements of the trade, lifts, alarm systems and several other items can be plant
- Structures, with some exceptions: dry docks and pipelines
- Land

Statutory inclusions

Computer software qualifies as plant by statute.

Case law

The courts tend to allow items as plant if they perform a function (eg moveable office partitions) in the particular trade, rather than form part of the setting within which the trade is carried on.

Machinery

Machinery also qualifies for allowances where machinery is given its ordinary every day meaning.

Writing down allowances (WDAs)

- 20% per annum on a reducing balance basis in main pool

  > Main pool includes cars with CO_2 emissions 160 g/km or less without private use

- WDA given on pool balance after adding current period additions and deducting current period disposals
- 20% × months/12 in a period that is not 12 months long
- Reduced WDAs can be claimed
- Expenditure on long life assets, integral features, thermal insulation and cars with CO_2 emissions over 160 g/km goes in a special rate pool. WDA is 10% per annum on a reducing balance basis
- Small balance (up to £1,000) on main pool and/or special rate pool can be given WDA equal to balance

> Deduct lower of
> (i) disposal proceeds
> (ii) original cost

First year allowances (FYAs)

- FYA of 100% available for expenditure on cars with CO_2 emissions 110 g/km or less
- Not pro-rated in short/long accounting periods

Annual Investment Allowance (AIA)

- All businesses are entitled to AIA of £100,000 per annum
- £100,000 maximum allowance is proportionately increased/reduced if period of account is not 12 months
- Allocate AIA to assets eligible for lowest rate of WDA
- Transfer balance after AIA to pool before main pool items (special rate pool items)
- Transfer balance after AIA to pool for same period WDAs
- Expenditure on plant and machinery (although not cars) is entitled to the AIA.

Balancing adjustments arise

| On cessation to deal with balances remaining after deduction of disposal proceeds. | When a non-pooled asset is sold. | When a column balance becomes negative. |

Expensive cars (acquired pre April 2009)/short life assets/private use assets

This will be a balancing charge

Short life assets (SLA)

- An **election** can be made to **depool assets.**
- Depooled assets must be disposed of within **8 years** of end of the period of acquisition.
- From a planning point of view depooling is useful if balancing allowances are expected.
- Conversely, in general, assets should not be depooled if they are likely to be sold within eight years for more than their tax written down values.

-Within two years of the end of the accounting period of acquisition (companies)
-31 Jan, 22 months from end of tax year (unincorporated businesses)

■ Otherwise the balance of expenditure must be transferred back to pool

Not cars

Private use assets

- Do not pool private use assets ■
- Show full value of asset/allowances in column
- Can only claim the business proportion of allowances

■ Assets used privately by a proprietor (not an employee) so not relevant to companies

Expensive cars (pre April 2009)

Expensive cars (£12,000+) acquired before 6.4.09 (1.4.09 companies) are dealt with separately and the WDA is restricted to £3,000 pa.

9: Assessable trading income

We have seen how to calculate the taxable trading profits for a business. We now see how these profits are allocated to tax years.

Again, this is a frequently examined topic.

Current year basis

The basis period for a tax year is normally the period of account ending in the year.

There are special rules which apply in the opening and closing years of a business and on a change of accounting date.

Opening years

Tax year	Basis period
1	Date of commencement to following 5 April.
2	(a) If no accounting date ends in year: 6 April - 5 April (b) If period of account ending in year is less than 12 months: first 12 months (c) Otherwise: 12 months to accounting date ending in Year 2
3	12 months to accounting date ending in year

Overlap profits

Any profits taxed twice are **overlap profits**. They may be deducted on a change of accounting date or on cessation.

| Current year basis | Commencement | Cessation | Change of accounting date |

Change of accounting date

When a change of accounting date results in

- one short period of account ending in a tax year, the basis period for that year is always the 12 months to the new accounting date.

- one long period of account ending in a tax year, the basis period for that year begins immediately after the end of the basis period for the previous year and ends on the new accounting date.

- two sets of accounts ending in a tax year, the basis period for that year begins immediately after the end of the basis period for the previous year and includes both sets of accounts.

- no sets of accounts, ending a tax year, there will be a notional accounting date in that tax year, and the basis period is the 12 months to this accounting date.

Final year

The basis period for the final year starts at the end of the basis period for the previous year and ends at cessation.

Any overlap profits not already relieved are deducted from the final year's profits.

> Overlap profits are relieved on a change of accounting date if more than 12 months worth of profit would otherwise be taxed in the year. They are relieved to bring the number of months worth of profit taxed in the year down to 12.

9: Assessable trading income

10: Trading losses

This is another key exam topic.

There is no general rule that sole traders can get relief for their losses. The conditions of a specific relief must be complied with. We look at these reliefs in this chapter.

Carry forward trade loss relief

A loss not otherwise relieved may be set against the first available profits of the same trade.

Losses **must** be set against the first available profits: they cannot be saved up until it suits the trader to use them.

A loss is calculated in exactly the same way as a profit. If there is a loss in a basis period the taxable trade profits for the tax year are nil - instead the loss is available in that tax year to be used as the trader chooses.

Losses may be carried forward for any number of years.

Incorporation

When a business is incorporated, pre-incorporation losses can be carried forward by the trader (not by the company) against income he receives from the company.

Against non-savings income, then savings income, then dividend income.

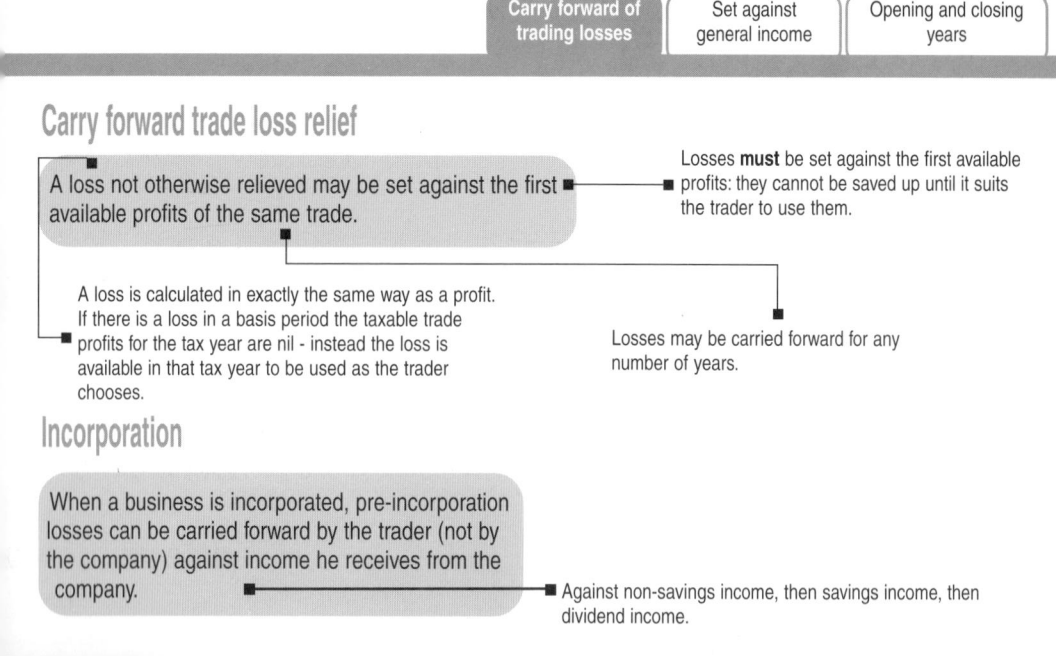

Losses in two overlapping basis periods are given to the earlier tax year only.

Relief against general income

Relief is against the **income of the tax year of the loss and/or the preceding tax year.**

Can extend the claim to net gains of the same year, less brought forward capital losses.

Example

Sue starts trading on 1.10.11. Her losses are:

y/e 30.9.12 £(50,000)
y/e 30.9.13 £(20,000)

Losses for the tax years are:

2011/12	£(25,000)
2012/13	£(50,000 – 25,000) = £(25,000)
2013/14	£(20,000)

Partial claims are not allowed: the whole loss must be set off, if there is income (or, if chosen, gains) to absorb it in the chosen tax year.

The trade must be carried on on a commercial basis with a view to the realisation of profits. Limit of £25,000 on set off for non-active traders

Exam focus

Before recommending relief against general income, consider whether it would lead to the waste of the personal allowance. This is often a significant tax planning point.

Opening years

A loss incurred in the first **four** years of trade can be set against general income of the **three** preceding years under early years trade losses relief

Relief is given in the earliest year first (FIFO)

Closing years

A loss incurred in the last **12 months** of trade can be set against trading profits in the year of cessation and in the **three** preceding years under terminal loss relief.

Relief is given in the latest year first (LIFO)

Computation of loss

Take the loss of the last tax year plus the proportion of the loss in the preceding tax year corresponding to the period from 12 months before cessation to 5 April.

Add unrelieved overlap profits to the loss in the last year.

11: Partnerships and limited liability partnerships

Partnerships are another key exam topic. The technique is to allocate the profits between the partners and then look at each partner independently.

Compute trading results for a partnership as a whole in the same way as you would compute the profits for a sole trader

then

Divide results for each period of account between partners

Remember to pro-rate the annual salary/interest if the period is not 12 months long.

First allocate salaries and interest on capital to the partners, then share the balance of profits among the partners according to the profit-sharing ratio for the period of account

When a partner joins, the first period of account for his own business runs from the date of joining to the firm's next accounting date. The normal basis period rules for opening years apply to him.

Each partner is taxed as if he were running his own business, and making profits and losses equal to his share of the firm's results for each period of account

When a partner leaves, the last period of account for his own business runs from the firm's most recent accounting date to the day he leaves. The normal cessation rules apply to him.

Loss reliefs

Partners are entitled to the same loss reliefs as sole traders:

1 Divide the loss for each period of account between the partners

2 Next calculate the loss for each tax year

3 Consider all available loss reliefs for each individual partner

Limited liability partnership (LLP)

In a LLP the liability of the partners is limited to the capital they contributed.

The amount of loss that a partner of a LLP can set off against general income comprising non-partnership income is restricted to the capital that the partner contributed up to a maximum of £25,000.

Notes

12: National insurance contributions

Although often overlooked, national insurance contributions represent a significant cost to taxpayers.

National insurance contributions will not be examined as a separate question, but may be examined in any question involving income tax or corporation tax.

NICs for employees	NICs for the self-employed

CLASS 1

Primary

Employees pay contributions of 12% of earnings between the primary earnings threshold and the upper earnings limit; 2% on earnings above the upper limit.

Not reduced by expenses or pension contributions

Secondary

Employers pay contributions of 13.8% on all earnings above the secondary earnings threshold.

CLASS 1A

Employers pay Class 1A contributions at 13.8% on most taxable benefits provided for their employees. Class 1A is payable on 19 July following the end of the tax year.

Exam focus

The earnings thresholds and the upper earnings limit will be given to you in the exam.

The self-employed pay Class 2 and Class 4 NICs.

Class 2

Class 2 are paid at a flat weekly rate. Paid by direct debit or on demand.

Exam focus

In questions which ask whether someone should trade as a sole trader or through a company (as a director) the cost of NICs often tips the balance in favour of being a sole trader.

Class 4

Class 4 NICs are 9% of any profits falling between a lower and an upper limit and 2% above upper limit. Class 4 NICs are collected at the same time as the associated income tax liability.

■ Profits are the taxable profits, as reduced by trading losses. Personal pension contributions do not reduce profits.

■ These limits will be given to you on the exam paper.

Notes

13: Computing chargeable gains

It is important that you can calculate chargeable gains realised by individuals and calculate their capital gains tax liability having dealt with losses and the offset of the annual exempt amount.

Chargeable persons, disposals and assets

Three elements are needed for a chargeable gain to arise.

1 A **chargeable disposal**: this includes sales, gifts and the destruction of assets. Transfer of assets on death is not chargeable.

2 A **chargeable person**: individuals are chargeable persons.

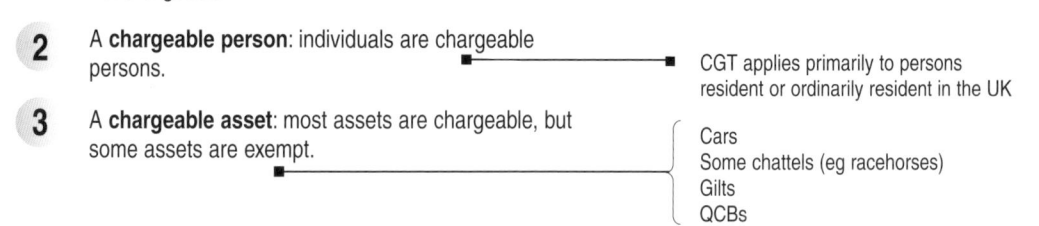

CGT applies primarily to persons resident or ordinarily resident in the UK

3 A **chargeable asset**: most assets are chargeable, but some assets are exempt.

Cars
Some chattels (eg racehorses)
Gilts
QCBs

Computation

	£
Compute a gain as follows:	
Proceeds	X ■
Less: Cost	(X) ■
Gain	X

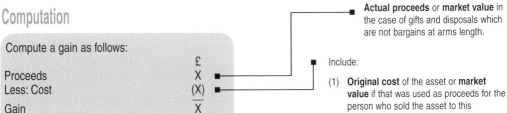

- **Actual proceeds** or **market value** in the case of gifts and disposals which are not bargains at arms length.

- Include:

  (1) **Original cost** of the asset or **market value** if that was used as proceeds for the person who sold the asset to this individual.

  (2) **Enhancement expenditure** which was reflected in the state and nature of the asset at the time of disposal or was on preserving the owner's legal right to the asset.

  (3) **Incidental costs** of **acquisition** and **disposal.**

Deduct allowable capital losses from gains in the tax year in which they arise (before deducting the annual exempt amount).

Allowable losses brought forward are only set off to reduce current year gains less current year allowable losses to the annual exempt amount.

Any loss which cannot be set off is carried forward to set against future gains.

Order of set off

Set off losses against gains not qualifying for entrepreneurs' relief first.

Example

Zoë made gains of £13,600 in 2011/12. She had brought forward capital losses of £8,000.

Brought forward capital losses of £3,000 will be set off in 2011/12. The remaining losses will be carried forward to 2012/13.

Deduct the annual CGT exempt amount of £10,600 (2011/12) to compute an individual's taxable gains.

from gains not qualifying for entrepreneurs' relief first

Rates

10% - entrepreneurs' relief gains

18% - within basic rate band

taxable income and gains qualifying for entrepreneurs' relief deducted first

28% - above basic rate limit

remember to extend limit by gross gift aid donations/ personal pension contributions

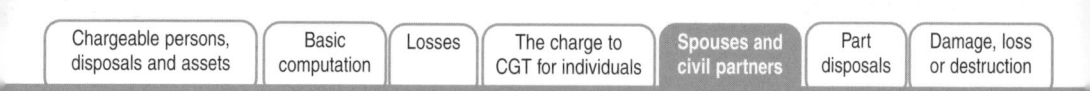

| Chargeable persons, disposals and assets | Basic computation | Losses | The charge to CGT for individuals | Spouses and civil partners | Part disposals | Damage, loss or destruction |

No gain/no loss disposals

Disposals between spouses and civil partners do not give rise to gains or losses.

When the second spouse/civil partner sells the asset, assume that he/she bought the asset for its original cost.

Part disposals

On a part disposal, you are only allowed to take part of the cost of the asset into account.

- Costs attributable solely to the part disposed of are taken into account in full ■
- For other costs, take into account A/(A+B) of the cost
  - A is the proceeds of the part sold
  - B is the market value of the part retained ■

Example

X owns land which originally cost £30,000. It sold a quarter interest in the land for £18,000. The incidental costs of disposal were £1,000. The market value of the three-quarter share remaining is estimated to be £36,000. What is the chargeable gain?

	£
Proceeds	18,000
Less: Incidental costs of disposal	(1,000)
	17,000
Less: $\dfrac{18,000}{18,000 + 36,000} \times 30,000$	(10,000)
	7,000

Damage

If an asset is damaged and compensation is received, then this will normally be treated as a part disposal.

If all the proceeds are used to restore the asset the taxpayer can elect to disregard the part disposal and deduct the proceeds from the cost of the asset.

Loss or destruction

If an asset is destroyed any compensation will normally be brought into an ordinary CGT disposal computation as proceeds.

If all the proceeds are applied for the replacement of the asset within 12 months, any gain can be deducted from the cost of the replacement asset.

If only part of the proceeds are applied, the gain is restricted to the proceeds not applied, and the remainder of the gain is deducted from the cost of the replacement asset.

14: Chattels and the principal private residence exemption

Topic List

Chattels

Wasting assets

Private residences

In this chapter we look at the rules which apply for calculating the gains on certain special types of asset.

Chattels

A chattel is an item of **tangible moveable property** (eg a painting).

⬇

Gains on chattels sold for gross proceeds of £6,000 or less are exempt.

⬇

The maximum gain on chattels sold for more than £6,000 is 5/3 (gross proceeds – £6,000).

⬇

Losses on chattels sold for under £6,000 are restricted by assuming the gross proceeds to be £6,000.

Wasting chattels

Wasting chattels are exempt from CGT unless capital allowances could have been claimed on them.

■ Chattels with a remaining estimated useful life of 50 years or less.

Wasting asset

A wasting asset is one with an estimated remaining useful life of 50 years or less and whose original value will fall over time.

Wasting assets have their cost written down over time on a straight line basis.

Exception

Assets eligible for capital allowances and used in a trade do not have their cost written down.

Example

Jo bought a copyright with a remaining life of 40 years for £10,000. He sold the copyright 15 years later for £30,000. Calculate the gain arising.

	£
Proceeds	30,000
Less: Cost (£10,000 × 25/40)	(6,250)
Gain	23,750

■ Number of years remaining

■ Number of years on acquisition

Principal private residence relief

A gain on the disposal of a PPR is wholly exempt where the owner has occupied the whole residence throughout his period of ownership.

Where occupation has been for only part of a period, the proportion of the gain exempted is

$$\text{Gain} \times \frac{\text{Period of occupation}}{\text{Total period of ownership}}$$

Periods of deemed occupation

- Absences of up to three years for any reason
- Absences while employed abroad
- Absences of up to four years while working elsewhere

These periods must normally be preceded and followed by a period of actual occupation

- The last 36 months of ownership of a residence is always treated as a period of deemed occupation.

- Provided that there is no other main residence at the time

Exam focus

Draw up a table of periods present or absent, exempt months and chargeable months. Check that the total of exempt and chargeable months is correct, to avoid making mistakes.

Business use

When part of residence is used exclusively for business purposes, that part of gain is taxable. Last 36 month exemption does not apply.

Letting exemption

A gain arising whilst a PPR is let is exempt up to the lower of:

1 £40,000

2 The amount of the PPR exemption

3 The gain in the let period

Permitted area

The private residence exemption covers a house plus up to half a hectare of grounds. A larger area may be allowed for substantial houses.

14: Chattels and the principal private residence exemption

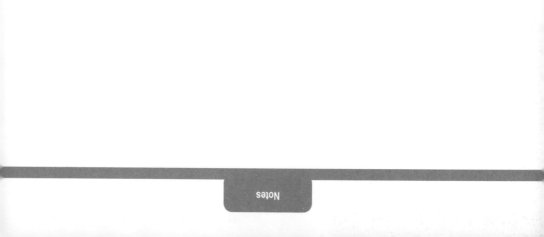

Notes

15: Business reliefs

Topic List

Rollover relief

Entrepreneurs' relief

Gift relief

Incorporation relief

In an exam question you should look out for the availability of various reliefs. However, do take care to ensure that you do not claim relief when you are not allowed to.

Taxpayers can claim to defer gains arising on the disposal of business assets that are being replaced if both the old and the new assets are on the list of eligible assets.

The new asset must be bought in the period starting 12 months before and ending 36 months after the disposal.

Exam focus

If a question mentions the sale of some business assets and the purchase of others, look out for rollover relief but do not just assume that it is available: the assets might be of the wrong type, eg moveable plant and machinery.

Eligible assets

- Land and buildings (including parts of buildings) occupied as well as used only for the purposes of the trade.
- Fixed (that is, immovable) plant and machinery.
- Goodwill

A depreciating asset is one with an expected life of 60 years or less (eg fixed plant and machinery).

Is the new asset a **depreciating** asset?
Is the new asset a **non-depreciating** asset?

For a non-depreciating asset the gain is deducted from the base cost of the new asset.

For a depreciating asset the gain is deferred until it crystallises at a later date.

If a part of the proceeds of the old asset are not reinvested, the gain is chargeable up to the amount not reinvested.

The gain crystallises on the earliest of:

1 the disposal of the replacement asset

2 ten years after the acquisition of the replacement asset

3 the date the replacement asset ceases to be used in the trade

Relief is proportionately restricted when an asset has not been used for trade purposes throughout its life.

If a non-depreciating qualifying asset is bought before the gain crystallises, the deferred gain may be rolled into the base cost of that asset.

Entrepreneurs' relief ■────────────■ Claim by 12 months from 31 January following tax year of disposal

Available for material disposal of business assets

⬇

Owned for one year prior to disposal or business has ceased within past three years and business owned at least one year prior to cessation

⬇

Tax net gains at 10%
Lifetime limit of £10m gains

Business assets

- Sole trader business/partnership
- Shares in 'personal' trading company owned by employee/officer

'Personal' trading company requires shareholding/voting rights of at least 5%

Must be the disposal of the whole or part of the business, not just individual assets if business continues

Gift relief

Gift relief may be claimed to defer gains arising on business assets.

↓

The gain is deducted from the recipient's base cost

↓

Any actual proceeds in excess of cost reduce the gain for which relief can be claimed.

Qualifying assets

- Assets used in a trade
- Shares and securities in trading company which is either unlisted or the donor's personal company

- If balance sheet of company contains non business assets gain eligible restricted to CBA/CA × gain

Incorporation relief

Incorporation relief applies when a business is incorporated as a going concern and all assets (or all except cash) are transferred to a company for consideration wholly or partly in shares.

Relief is **automatic** if conditions satisfied (but can be disapplied).

The gain is deducted from the base cost of the shares.

If only a proportion of the consideration for incorporation is in the form of shares only that proportion of the gain can be relieved.

16: Shares and securities

The matching rules for shares and securities are vitally important. If you do not know the matching rules you will not be able to compute a gain on the disposal of shares.

The matching rules for shares held by an individual are different to the matching rules for shares held by a company. Take care not to confuse the two.

Matching rules for individuals

Disposals by individual shareholders are matched with acquisitions in the following order:

- Same day acquisitions
- Acquisitions within the following 30 days
- Any shares in the share pool

Exam focus

Learn the 'matching rules' because a crucial first step to getting a shares question right is to correctly match the shares sold to the original shares purchased.

The computation

The computation is proceeds less cost.

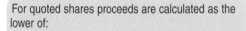

For quoted shares proceeds are calculated as the lower of:

- 1/4 up, and
- Mid bargain

The share pool

The share pool is kept in two columns:

1 The **number** of shares

2 The **cost**

On a disposal the cost is calculated on a pro-rata basis.

Reorganisations and takeovers

- Apportion the cost of the old shares to the new assets received in proportion to their values.
- Where the new assets include cash, compute a chargeable gain using the cash received and the part of the cost of the old shares apportioned to that cash.
- Takeover must be for bona fide commercial reasons and not for tax avoidance for this treatment to apply.

Rights issues

- Rights issue shares are acquired for payment.
- Add the numbers of shares to the share pool and add the cost of the rights shares.

Bonus issues

- Bonus issue shares are acquired at no cost.
- Add the number of shares to the share pool.

17: Self-assessment and payment of tax by individuals

Topic List

Returns

Records and appeals

Payment of tax

Penalties

This is a key exam topic. It may appear as part of any personal tax question.

Filing date

The latest filing date for filing a 2011/12 tax return is:

(1) 31 October 2012 (paper)

Exception: if notice after 31 July 2012, latest filing date is end of 3 months after notice.

(2) 31 January 2013 (electronic)

Exception: if notice after 31 October 2012, latest filing date is end of 3 months after notice.

Compliance checks

HMRC randomly select returns to check. They also select returns where there is an identified tax risk.

HMRC may check a return provided they give notice by a year after:

(1) The actual filing date (if on or before due filing date)

(2) The 31 January, 30 April, 31 July or 31 October next following the actual filing date of the return (if filed late).

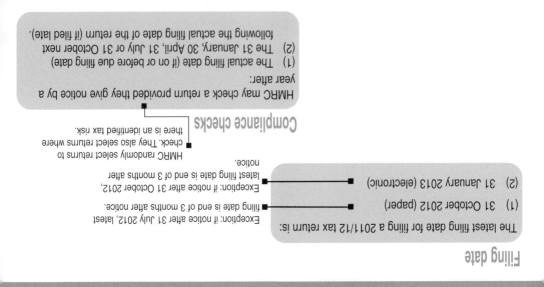

Records

Records must, in general, be kept until the later of:

(1) Five years after the 31 January following the tax year concerned (where the taxpayer is in business); or

(2) One year after the 31 January following the tax year, otherwise

Appeals

- A taxpayer may appeal against:
    - any assessment, except a self-assessment
    - an amendment to a self-assessment or a disallowance of a claim or election, following a compliance check or discovery
    - penalties
- The appeal may be settled by internal review. If not, the hearing is before Tax Tribunal.

Powers

- HMRC can demand that taxpayers and, in certain cases, their accountants produce information (eg documents).
- HMRC may make assessments to recover tax due and determinations which effectively force the filing of a return.

17: Self-assessment and payment of tax by individuals

Returns	Records and appeals	**Payment of tax**	Penalties

Payment of tax

Payments on account (POA) of income tax and Class 4 NICs must be made on 31 January in tax year and on the following 31 July.

The final payment of income tax and Class 4 NICs must be paid on 31 January following the tax year.

All CGT is due on 31 January following the tax year.

Each POA is 50% of the prior tax year's income tax and Class 4 NIC liability less tax suffered at source (de minimis limits £1,000, 80%)

Interest

Interest runs on:

(1) POAs from the normal due dates (31 Jan and 31 July).

(2) Any final payment and CGT from the later of:
   (i) 31 January following tax year
   (ii) Three months after the notice to file a tax return was issued

Penalties for errors

- Common penalty regime for IT, NICs, CT and VAT

- Imposed for inaccurate return leading to understatement of tax, false or increased loss, false or increased repayment of tax

- Error may be careless, deliberate but not concealed, or deliberate and concealed

Maximum penalty based on Potential Lost Revenues (PLR):

- 100% if deliberate and concealed

- 70% if deliberate but not concealed

- 30% if careless

Penalties can be reduced by disclosure (eg 0% for careless error with unprompted disclosure)

Penalties for late notification

- Common penalty regime for IT, NICs, PAYE, CGT, CT and VAT
- Failure may be careless, deliberate but not concealed, or deliberate and concealed
  - Maximum penalty based on PLR as for penalties for error
  - Reduced penalties for disclosure: eg 0% if careless failure with unprompted disclosure within 12 months

Penalty for failure to keep records

£3,000 per tax year/accounting period

Penalties for late filing

The maximum penalties for delivering a return after the filing due date are:

(1)	Return up to 3 months late	£100
(2)	Return over 3 months late	As (1) plus £10 daily penalty (max 90 days)
(3)	Return over 6 months late	As (1) and (2) plus greater of 5% of tax and £300
(4)	Return over 12 months late	As (1), (2), (3) plus greater of % of tax (conduct related) and £300

Penalties for late payment

(1) Penalty date is 30 days after due date

(2) Penalty of 5% of unpaid tax at penalty date if payment not more than 5 months after penalty date

(3) Penalty of 5% of unpaid tax at 5 months after penalty date if payment between 5 months and 11 months of penalty date

(4) Penalty of 5% of unpaid tax at 11 months after penalty date if payment more than 11 months after penalty date

(5) Does not apply to payments on account

17: Self-assessment and payment of tax by individuals

Notes

18: Inheritance tax

Topic List

Scope/basic principles

CLTs and PETs

Death estate

Transfer of nil rate band

Exemptions

Payment of IHT

Inheritance tax is a tax on transfer of wealth (gifts). It will be examined for between 5 and 15 marks in any of Questions 3, 4 or 5.

Scope of inheritance tax

Transfer of value

By individuals

Lifetime or death

For F6, a gift

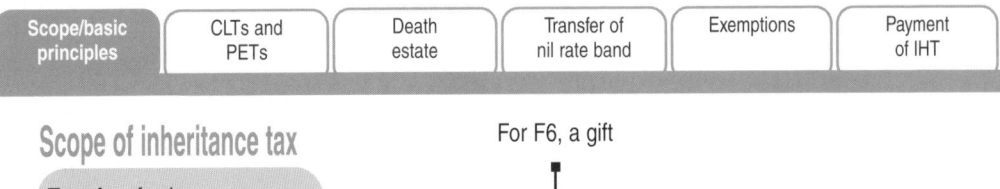

Transfer of value

A gratuitous disposition which results in an individual being worse off.

Diminution in value

Usually = gift but watch out for unquoted shares (before/after)

The value of the transfer is always the loss to the donor.

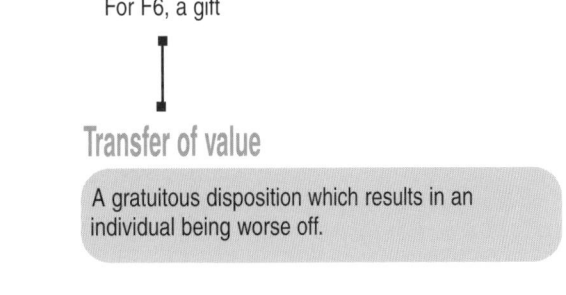

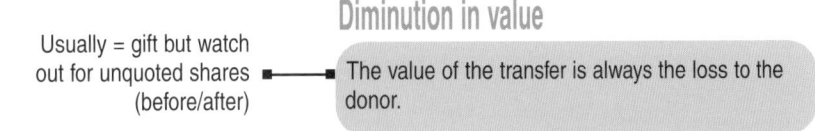

7 year accumulation principle

Need to look back 7 years from chargeable transfer to see if any chargeable transfers use up available nil rate band

2011/12 £325,000

Chargeable transfer

Any transfer which is not an exempt transfer.

Chargeable lifetime transfer (CLT) - immediate charge to tax. Gift to trust.

Potentially exempt transfer (PET) only chargeable if donor does not survive 7 years - treat as exempt until death. Gift to individual (except spouse/civil partner).

Chargeable transfer on death.

Chargeable lifetime transfers (CLTs)

IHT charged at date of gift at 20% if exceeds nil rate band at date of gift. ◄─────

─── gross up (20/80) if donor pays lifetime tax as he has lost both the gift and the IHT paid.

Additional tax on death

The IHT on death on a CLT made in 7 years before death is calculated as follows:

(1) Take into account all chargeable transfers in 7 yrs before this transfer (including PETs which have become chargeable)

(2) Calculate the tax at 40% on excess of the gross CLT over nil rate band at death

(3) Deduct taper relief if death between 3-7 yrs after transfer

(4) Deduct lifetime tax - but no repayment if exceeds tapered death tax

Exam focus

When you have grossed up a transfer, you can check your figures by computing the 20% tax on the gross transfer.

Potentially Exempt Transfers (PETs)

Treat as exempt during lifetime of donor ■———————■ if donor does survive 7 years from transfer, PET is exempt transfer

Tax on death

IHT on a PET made in 7 years before death is calculated as follows:

(1) Take into account all chargeable transfers in 7 yrs before this transfer (including other PETs which have become chargeable)

(2) Calculate tax @ 40% on excess over nil rate band at death

(3) Deduct taper relief if death between 3-7 yrs after transfer

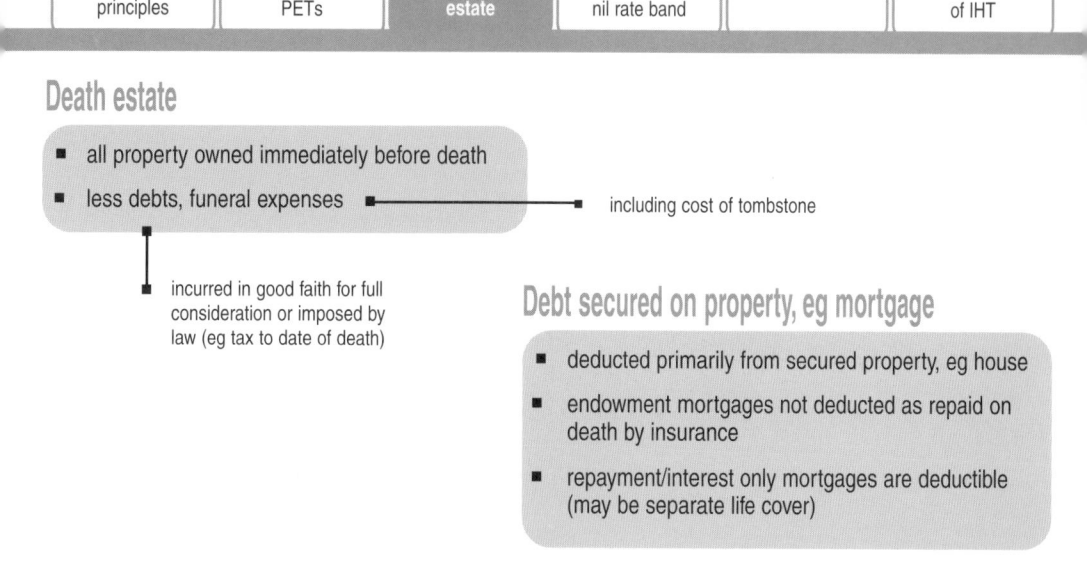

Death estate

- all property owned immediately before death
- less debts, funeral expenses ● ———————————— including cost of tombstone

● incurred in good faith for full consideration or imposed by law (eg tax to date of death)

Debt secured on property, eg mortgage

- deducted primarily from secured property, eg house
- endowment mortgages not deducted as repaid on death by insurance
- repayment/interest only mortgages are deductible (may be separate life cover)

Tax on death estate

(1) Take into account all transfers in 7 years before death (including PETs which have become chargeable).

(2) Calculate the tax at 40% on excess over nil rate band at death.

Transfer of unused nil rate band

- individual (A) dies
- A had spouse/civil partner (B) who died before A
- B had unused nil rate band on death

Effect

- Nil rate band of A increased by unused nil rate band of B
- Affects additional tax on CLTs, tax on PETs and death estate
- Scale up if nil rate band increased between B's death and A's death

Claim

Within 2 years of end of month of A's death by A's PRs.

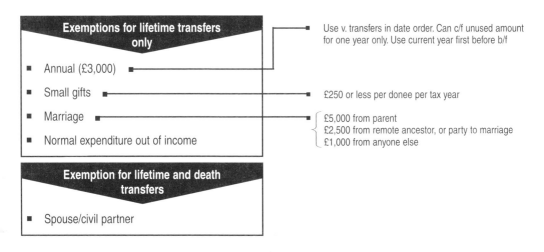

Exemptions for lifetime transfers only

- Annual (£3,000) — Use v. transfers in date order. Can c/f unused amount for one year only. Use current year first before b/f

- Small gifts — £250 or less per donee per tax year

- Marriage —
  - £5,000 from parent
  - £2,500 from remote ancestor, or party to marriage
  - £1,000 from anyone else

- Normal expenditure out of income

Exemption for lifetime and death transfers

- Spouse/civil partner

Payment of IHT

Event	Liability to pay tax	Due date
CLT - lifetime tax	Donor unless trustees agree to pay	Later of (1) 30 April just after end of tax year (2) 6 months after end of month of transfer
CLT - death tax	Trustees	6 months from end of month of donor's death
PET	Donee	6 months from end of month of donor's death
Death estate	PRs	Earlier of (1) Delivery of account (2) 6 months from end of month of donor's death

19: Computing taxable total profits

Topic List

In this chapter we will cover the structure of the computation of taxable total profits. This is an essential part of your examination as Question 2 is on corporation tax.

Period of account

A period of account is the period for which accounts are prepared.

Accounting period

An accounting period is the period for which corporation tax is charged.

An accounting period can never exceed 12 months. If a company prepares accounts for a period exceeding twelve months, the period of account must be split into two accounting periods.

- It starts when the company starts to trade, or immediately after the end of the previous accounting period.

- It ends 12 months after it starts or, if earlier, when the period of account ends.

The first 12 months form the first accounting period

The remaining months form the second accounting period

Residence

A company is resident in the UK if it is incorporated in the UK or if its central management and control are in the UK.

A UK resident company is subject to UK corporation tax on its worldwide profits.

Taxable total profits

A company's taxable total profits are arrived at by aggregating its various sources of income and chargeable gains (total profits) and then deducting gift aid donations and certain losses.

Profits of trades ■

Interest from non-trading loan relationships ■
(eg bank/building society interest)

Income from foreign possessions ■

Any other profits ■

Income from land and buildings in the UK ■

Proforma for calculating taxable total profits

	£
■ Trading profits	X
■ Investment income	X
■ Foreign income	X
■ Miscellaneous income	X
■ Property business income	X
Chargeable gains	X
Total profits	X
Less: losses deductible from total profits	(X)
Less: gift aid donations	(X)
Taxable total profits	X

Dividends from other companies (UK and overseas) are not included in taxable total profits.

Trading profits

The computation of trading profits follows income tax principles.

Remember there is no disallowance of expenditure or restriction of capital allowances for private use.

Proforma

	£	£
Net profit per accounts		X
Add expenditure not allowed for tax purposes		X
		X
Deduct		
Income not taxable as trading income	X	
Expenditure not charged in the accounts but allowable for tax	X	
Capital allowances	X	
		(X)
Taxable trading profits		X

Property business income

The computation of property business income follows income tax principles.

Exception: Interest on a loan taken out to buy property is dealt with under the loan relationship rules, not as part of the property business.

Property business losses

Set against total profits of the company for the same accounting period, then carry the excess forward as a property business loss.

Loan relationships

A company that borrows or invests money has a loan relationship.

Trading loan relationship

- Held for trade purposes (eg debentures issued for trade purposes)
- Costs (eg interest) accruing are deductible trading income expenses
- Income accruing (eg interest income) is taxable as trading income.

Non-trading loan relationship

- Held for non-trade purposes (eg building society account held for investment purposes)
- Tax income accruing as interest income
- Deduct expenses accruing from the pool of interest income.

  - Net deficits are not examinable

Long period of account (> 12 months)

The first 12 months form the first accounting period

The remaining months form the second accounting period

Example

If A Ltd prepares accounts for the fifteen months to 31.12.11, there will be one 12 month accounting period to 30.9.11 and a second three month accounting period to 31.12.11.

Division of profits

Divide profits between the accounting periods as follows:

- Trading income: time apportion the amount before capital allowances
- Compute capital allowances separately for each period
- Property business income: time apportion
- Other income: allocate to period in which it accrues
- Miscellaneous income: time apportion
- Gains: allocate to the period in which they are realised
- Gift aid donations: allocate to the period in which they are paid

Notes

20: Computing the corporation tax liability

In this chapter we will cover the calculation of the corporation tax liability. This too is an essential part of your examination.

The charge to corporation tax | Associated companies

Rates

Rates of corporation tax (CT) are:

- Set for financial years ■
- Dependent on the level of augmented profits

A financial year runs from 1 April in one year to 31 March in the next. Financial Year 2011 (FY 2011) runs from 1 April 2011 to 31 March 2012.

If there is a change in the rate of CT, and a company's accounting period does not fall entirely into one financial year, the taxable total profits and augmented profits of the period are time apportioned to the two financial years.

Augmented profits

Augmented profits are taxable total profits plus the grossed up amount of dividends (FII) received from outside 51% group.

The **main rate** (FY 2011 – 26%) of CT applies if augmented profits exceed the upper limit.

The **small profits rate** (FY 2011 – 20%) applies if augmented profits are below the lower limit.

Marginal relief is given if augmented profits fall between the upper and lower limits

Exam focus

The marginal relief formula will be given to you in the exam.

- It is: standard fraction × (Upper limit − augmented profits) × $\dfrac{\text{taxable total profits}}{\text{augmented profits}}$

20: Computing the corporation tax liability

Upper and lower limits

The lower and upper limits are:

- Multiplied by months/12 for short accounting periods
- Shared equally between the number of 'associated' companies in the group

Companies under common control

Exclude dormant companies but include trading non-resident companies

Example

A Ltd, which has one associated company, prepares accounts for the nine months to 31.3.12. The upper limit for this period is

$$9/12 \times \frac{£1,500,000}{2} = £562,500$$

21: Chargeable gains for companies

Topic List

Calculation of chargeable gains

Disposal of shares

Rollover relief

This chapter deals with calculating chargeable gains for companies.

A key area is the rules for the disposal of shares and securities.

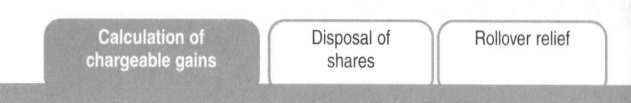
Computation

Compute a gain as follows:

	£
Proceeds	X
Less: allowable cost	(X)
Less: indexation allowance	(X)
Chargeable gain	X

(1) Cannot create or increase a loss

(2) Round to 3 decimal places before multiplying by cost.

$$\frac{\text{RPI for month of disposal} - \text{RPI for month of acquisition}}{\text{RPI for month of acquisition}}$$

1. Include in total profits, and so charged to corporation tax
2. No annual exempt amount

Shares and securities

For company shareholders disposals of shares and securities are matched with acquisitions in the following order.

(i) Shares acquired on the same day

(ii) Shares acquired in the previous nine days, taking earlier acquisitions first

(iii) Shares from the FA 1985 pool

The FA 1985 pool is kept in three columns:

1 The **number** of shares

2 The **cost**

3 The **indexed cost**

Do not round indexation to 3 decimal places after April 1985.

The indexation allowance is the indexed cost taken out of the indexed cost column minus the cost taken out of the cost column.

Operative event

Operative events are acquisitions and disposals (apart from bonus issues)

At each operative event

(1) Increase the indexed cost column by the indexed rise since the date of the last operative event, then

(2) Add the cost of any shares acquired to both the cost/indexed cost columns, or

(3) Deduct a pro-rata slice from the cost/indexed cost columns in respect of any shares disposed of.

Reorganisations and takeovers

- Apportion the cost and indexed cost of the old shares to the new assets received in proportion to their values.

- Where the new assets include cash, compute a chargeable gain using the cash received and the parts of the cost and indexed cost of the old shares apportioned to that cash.

- If just a takeover qualifying for the 'paper for paper' treatment, the cost and indexed cost of the original holding is passed onto the new holding which now takes its place.

Companies can claim to defer gains arising on the disposal of business assets that are being replaced if:

1 The old and the new assets are used in the trade of the company

2 The old and the new assets are on the list of qualifying assets

3 The new asset is bought in the period starting 12 months before and ending 36 months after the disposal

Eligible assets

- Land and buildings (including parts of buildings) occupied as well as used only for the purposes of the trade.

- Fixed (that is, immovable) plant and machinery.

A depreciating asset is one with an expected life of 60 years or less (eg fixed plant and machinery).

Is the new asset a **depreciating** asset?
Is the new asset a **non-depreciating** asset?

For a non-depreciating asset the gain is deducted from the base cost of the new asset.

For a depreciating asset the gain is deferred until it crystallises at a later date.

If a part of the proceeds of the old asset are not reinvested, the gain is chargeable up to the amount not reinvested.

The gain crystallises on the earliest of:

1 The disposal of the replacement asset

2 Ten years after the acquisition of the replacement asset

3 The date the replacement asset ceases to be used in the trade

Relief is proportionately restricted when an asset has not been used for trade purposes throughout its life.

If a non-depreciating qualifying asset is bought before the gain crystallises, the deferred gain may be rolled into the base cost of that asset.

Notes

22: Losses

Topic List

Trading losses

Non-trading losses

In this chapter we will see how a single company may obtain tax relief for its trading and non-trading losses. Losses are a key topic area for exam purposes. The best way of learning how to deal with losses is to practise questions involving losses in the BPP Learning Media Practice and Revision Kit.

Trading losses

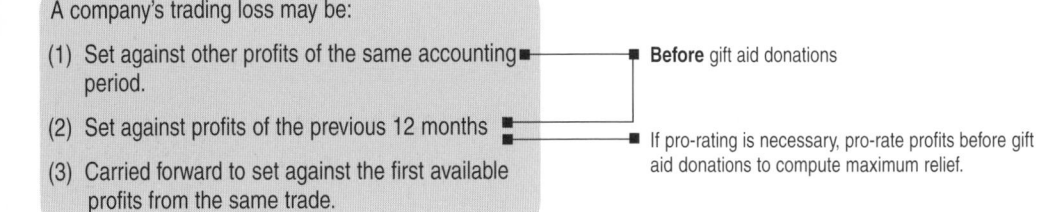

A company's trading loss may be:

(1) Set against other profits of the same accounting period.

(2) Set against profits of the previous 12 months

(3) Carried forward to set against the first available profits from the same trade.

Before gift aid donations

If pro-rating is necessary, pro-rate profits before gift aid donations to compute maximum relief.

Reliefs (1) and (2) need to be claimed. A company can choose to claim relief (1) only (ie relief (1) but not relief (2)). However, if relief (2) is to be claimed, relief (1) must be claimed first. Relief (3) is given automatically to any loss not relieved under (1) or (2).

Cessation of trade

- The 12 month carry back period in (2) above is extended to 36 months where the trading loss arose in the 12 months prior to the cessation of trade.
- Gift aid donations are unrelieved.

The choice between reliefs

- Relieve losses at the highest possible marginal tax rate
- Consider timing: earlier relief is better than later relief

Trading losses

Non-trading losses

Non-trading losses

Capital losses

Capital losses can only be set against capital gains in current or future accounting periods. They must be set against the first available gains.

Property business income

Property business losses are first set against total profits for the current period. Any excess is then carried forward as though it were a property business loss arising in a later period.

23: Groups

When presented with a group question in the exam always establish the percentage holding at each level and the effective interest of the holding company in each subsidiary. These figures will determine the reliefs available.

Group relief allows the losses of one group company to be set against the taxable total profits of another.

Group relief group

For a group relief group to exist one company must have a 75% effective interest in the other, or there must be a third company which has a 75% effective interest in both.

Losses available to surrender

Trading losses
Excess property business losses
Excess gift aid donations

Non-UK resident companies may be included within the group although losses cannot normally be surrendered to/from UK residents.

Capital losses cannot be group relieved.

Exam focus

Give group relief where it will save most tax: firstly to companies in the marginal relief band (marginal rate 27.5%), then to companies paying the 26% rate, then to companies paying at the 20% rate.

Group relief is given before relief for any amounts brought back from later periods.

A claim for group relief is normally made on the claimant company's tax return. It is ineffective unless notice of consent is also given by the surrendering company.

Available profits

Profits available to absorb group relief are total profits less gift aid donations and current and brought forward losses.

Corresponding accounting periods

Group relief is strictly a current period relief. If accounting periods do not coincide, the profits and losses must be time-apportioned. Only the profits and losses of the period of overlap may be matched up.

Capital gains group

A capital gains group starts with the top company (which must be included). It carries on down while there is a 75% holding at each level and the effective interest of the top company is over 50%.

No gain/loss arises when an asset is transferred within a capital gains group.

Two members of a capital gains group can elect to transfer gains/losses between them.

Rollover relief

All members of a capital gains group may be treated as a single unit for the purpose of rollover relief.

24: Overseas matters for companies

Topic List

Overseas operations

Double tax relief

Transfer pricing

Questions on the overseas aspects of corporation tax are likely to require you to prepare a CT computation. Practise using a standard format for DTR computations, with columns (or rows) for corporation tax, and DTR and rows (or columns) for the different sources of profits. This will help ensure that you get the computation right.

A UK resident company is subject to corporation tax on its worldwide profits.

The company may trade overseas through a branch or subsidiary.

Overseas profits may be taxable as trading income, investment income or foreign income, or as chargeable gains.

If overseas profits are subject to both overseas and UK taxation **double tax relief** may be available to reduce the tax arising.

Overseas branch

- Useful if expect losses.
- Branch profits taxed as trading income.
- Relief is automatically available for branch losses.

Overseas subsidiary

- Can be useful if profits taxed at lower rate abroad.
- No group relief for losses.
- Dividends received by UK parent usually not taxable.

Credit relief ■————————————————————————■ This is the only type of DTR examinable at F6

Credit relief relieves overseas tax on overseas profits up to the **lower** of the:

(a) UK tax on the overseas income
(b) Overseas tax on the overseas income

Computation

Include:

- **Gross** overseas income in CT computation.
- Gross up for withholding tax.

Deduct gift aid donation/losses from UK income and then from foreign income suffering lowest tax rate.

Transfer
pricing

Double
tax relief

Overseas
operations

Transfer pricing

Under the transfer pricing legislation a company may be deemed to have bought/sold goods at their market value. This anti-avoidance provision is particularly aimed at preventing UK companies from diverting profits to other group members which may pay tax at a lower rate.

Companies must self-assess their liability to tax under the transfer pricing rules and pay any corporation tax due.

25: Self-assessment and payment of tax by companies

In this chapter we look at both the administration of corporation tax (CT) and when that tax must be paid. This is a key exam topic.

Returns

A company must normally file its CT return by the due filing date which is the later of:

- Twelve months after the end of the period to which the return relates
- Three months after a notice requiring the return was issued

Compliance checks

Notice to check a return must be given by 12 months after the later of:

- The actual filing date if filed on or before due filing date
- The 31 January, 30 April, 31 July or 31 October next following the actual filing date if filed late

Records must generally be kept for six years from the end of the accounting period concerned.

Late filing of Return

- Initial fixed penalty is £100 rising to £200 if the return is more than three months late
- Fixed penalties rise to £500 and £1,000 if the return for each of the two preceding periods was also late
- If the return was between 6 and 12 months late there is an additional tax geared penalty of 10% of the tax unpaid six months after the filing date
- If the return is over 12 months late the tax geared penalty is 20% of the tax unpaid six months after the filing date

Common penalty regime applies for errors on return/late notification of chargeability

Due dates

Any company that pays CT at the main rate

- 'Large' companies must pay their anticipated CT liability in quarterly instalments.
- Other companies must pay their CT liability nine months and one day after the end of the accounting period (AP)

Quarterly instalments

- For a 12 month AP instalments are due in:
  - months 7 and 10 in the period
  - months 1 and 4 in the following period
- For an AP less than 12 months instalments are due in:
  - month 7 of the period
  - then at 3 monthly intervals
  - final payment in month 4 of next period
  - amount of instalment is $3 \times CT/n$ where n is length of AP and CT is amount due in instalments
- Instalments are due on 14th day of the month

Interest runs from the due date. Overpaid tax earns interest from the date it is paid. The position is looked at cumulatively after the date for each instalment.

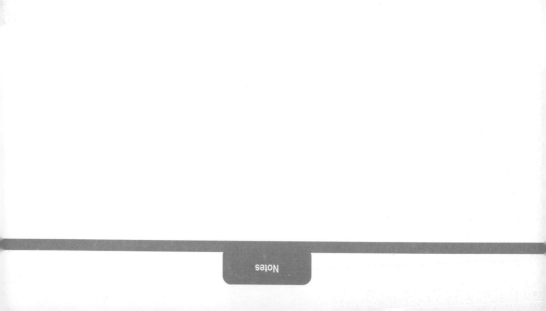

Notes

26: An introduction to VAT

Topic List

Scope of VAT

Zero-rated, exempt and taxable supplies

Registration

Accounting and administration

Valuation of supplies

Deduction of input tax

VAT is a tax with many detailed rules.

At least 10 marks will be given for VAT, and it may be included as part of question 1 or 2, or as a separate question.

VAT is a tax on revenue/turnover, not on profits. It is imposed at each stage in a chain of sales, in such a way that the burden falls on the final consumer.

VAT applies to **taxable supplies** of goods or services made in the UK by a **taxable person** in the course of a business.

A taxable supply is a supply of goods or services made in the UK other than an exempt supply

A taxable person is a person that is registered or ought to be registered

Supplies

A taxable supply is either standard rated or zero-rated.

Zero-rated supplies are taxed at 0%.

Standard rated supplies are normally taxed at 20%.

An exempt supply is not chargeable to VAT.

Gift of goods

Normally a supply at cost but business gifts are not supplies if:

- The cost to the donor is £50 or less, or
- The gift is a sample (unlimited numbers)

1 Zero-rated supplies

Taxable at 0%
Can recover input VAT
Eg food, books and newspapers

2 Exempt supplies

Not taxable
Cannot recover input VAT
Eg insurance, education and health services

3 Standard rated supplies

Taxable, normally at 20% (5% in some cases)
All supplies which are not zero-rated or exempt

Compulsory registration

Must register if:

1. the value of taxable supplies exceeds the registration limit in any past period of up to 12 calendar months, or

2. there are reasonable grounds for believing that the value of taxable supplies will exceed the registration limit in the next 30 days.

Notification required within 30 days of the end of the 12 month period. **Registration** takes effect from the end of the month following the 12 month period.

Notification required by the end of the 30 day period. **Registration** takes effect from the beginning of that period.

Voluntary registration

Advantages

☑ Input VAT can be reclaimed
☑ The impression of a substantial business is given

Disadvantages

☒ Increased administration
☒ Penalties if VAT/return is late
☒ Increased cost for non-registered customers

The registration limit is currently £73,000.
(This limit will be given to you in the exam.)

Exam focus

The examiner may favour VAT questions requiring advice to new traders (should they register, etc).

Voluntary deregistration

Can deregister voluntarily if the value of taxable supplies in the following one year period will not exceed £71,000.

VAT is due on all inventory and capital assets on which input VAT was claimed.

■ EXCEPTIONS

1 If VAT does not exceed £1,000 it need not be paid

2 VAT is not due if the business is sold as a going concern to another taxable person

Pre-registration input VAT

Reclaimable VAT is:

1. VAT on goods bought in the four years prior to registration and still held at the date of registration

2. VAT on services supplied in the six months before registration

Group registration

Available to companies under **common control**.

Representative member accounts for all VAT.

Simplifies VAT accounting	All members jointly and severally liable for VAT

No VAT on supplies between group members.

Reduces VAT accounting	Improves cash flow

Any company can be **EXCLUDED** from group.

Consider excluding companies making zero-rated supplies.

VAT period

A trader accounts for VAT for each **VAT period**. Periods are normally three months long, but they may last for one month or 12 months. A VAT return is completed for each period.

VAT returns completed in paper form, must be submitted, along with the VAT due, within one month of the end of the period. Many businesses must now file and pay electronically which extends the usual time limit by seven days.

Substantial traders

If a trader does not make monthly returns, and the total VAT liability over 12 months to the end of a VAT period exceeds £2,000,000, he must make payments on account of each quarter's VAT liability during the quarter.

Tax point

Each supply is treated as taking place on the **tax point**.

Basic tax point

Date on which goods removed/made available to customer.

Actual tax point

Date invoice issued or payment made if before basic tax point

Alternatively, the invoice date, if invoice issued within 14 days after basic tax point

Administration

- Local VAT offices carry out general administration, advise taxable persons and check that the law is being properly applied.
- If HMRC are not satisfied with the figures supplied by a trader, they can issue assessments for the VAT which they believe to be due.
- Most decisions by HMRC can be appealed against. Appeals are heard by Tax Tribunal.

Value of supply

The value of a supply is the VAT-exclusive price.

Value + VAT = consideration

The VAT proportion of the consideration is the 'VAT fraction'

$$\frac{20}{120} = \frac{1}{6}$$

Example

If total consideration is £240, the VAT proportion is

£40 (240 × $\frac{1}{6}$)

Discounts

Where a discount is offered for prompt payment, VAT is always chargeable on the discounted amount.

Non-deductible VAT

- VAT on motor cars not wholly used for business purposes.
- VAT on business entertaining (except overseas customers).
- VAT on domestic accommodation for directors.
- VAT on non-business items.

Impairment losses (Bad debt relief)

- Claim within four years and six months
- Must be over 6 months old
- Must be written off in creditor's accounts
- Attribute payments on account in chronological order

From when payment is due

Fuel

VAT on:
- Fuel used for business purposes: fully deductible
- Fuel used for **private purposes**: fully deductible but account for output VAT based on a set scale figure

Based on CO_2 emissions

Where cost of fuel used for private purposes is not fully reimbursed to business

27: Further aspects of VAT

Topic List

VAT invoices and records

Penalties

Overseas aspects

Special schemes

For exam purposes, it is again important that you learn the detailed rules covered in this chapter. VAT will be the subject of at least 10 marks.

Invoices: required details

- Name, address and VAT no of supplier
- Name and address of customer
- Invoice no, date of issue and tax point
- Details of type of supply and the goods/services supplied
- For each supply: the quantity, the unit price, VAT rate and the VAT exclusive amount
- The rate of any cash discount
- The total invoice price excl. VAT (with separate totals for zero rated and exempt supplies)
- Each VAT rate and the total VAT

VAT invoices are not required for payments of up to £25 (including VAT) which are for telephone calls or car park fees or made through cash operated machines.

Less detailed invoices may be issued by retailer where the invoice is for up to £250 (incl VAT).

Records

VAT records must be kept for six years

Records must be kept up to date and in a way which allows:

- The calculations of VAT due
- Officers of HMRC to check the figures on VAT returns

Default surcharge

First late return/payment commences **surcharge period,** then:

Default involving late payment of VAT in the surcharge period	Surcharge as a percentage of the VAT outstanding at the due date
First	2%
Second	5%
Third	10%
Fourth and over	15%

2% and 5% surcharges are not normally demanded unless the amount due would be at least £400. For the 10% or 15% surcharges a minimum of £30 is payable.

Every time there is a default, the surcharge period is extended to the anniversary of the end of the default period.

Errors

Common penalty regime applies for errors on returns

Errors not exceeding greater of
- £10,000 (net error); or
- 1% × net VAT turnover for return period (max £50,000)

may be corrected on the next return. Other errors to be notified in writing, eg letter.
Penalties for error may be imposed in both cases.

Interest on unpaid VAT

Interest is charged on VAT which was or could have been assessed. It runs from when the VAT should have been paid to when it is paid. This period cannot exceed three years.

Outside the EU – goods

Imports of goods from outside the EU are subject to VAT at the same rate as on a supply within the UK.

Exports of goods to outside the EU are zero-rated.

Inside the EU – goods

When a taxable person supplies goods to a customer in another EU country, the supply is zero rated if the customer is VAT registered.

When goods are supplied to a registered trader in the UK from within the EU, VAT (calculated using UK rates) is due and shown on the next VAT return by the UK buyer of the goods.

Tax point earlier of:
- 15th of month following acquisition;
- invoice date.

Inside the EU – services

VAT treatment generally as for supply of goods.

Tax point earlier of time of service:
- completed;
- paid for.

Outside the EU – services

Import of services from outside EU – same as for goods.

Export of services to outside EU – outside scope of VAT.

Annual accounting scheme

- Annual taxable turnover must not exceed £1,350,000 (excl. VAT)
- Annual VAT return
- Traders normally have to make interim payments on account of their VAT liability during the year by direct debits

Advantages

- ☑ Only one VAT return each year so fewer occasions to trigger a default surcharge.
- ☑ Ability to manage cash flow more accurately.
- ☑ No need for quarterly calculations for input tax recovery.

Disadvantages

- ☒ Need to monitor future taxable supplies to ensure turnover limit not exceeded.
- ☒ Timing of payments have less correlation to turnover (and hence cash received).
- ☒ Payments based on previous year's turnover may not reflect current year turnover.

Cash accounting scheme

- Account for VAT on basis cash paid/received.
- Annual taxable turnover must not exceed £1,350,000 (excl VAT).
- To join, all VAT returns/payments must be up to date (or arrangements have been made to pay outstanding VAT by instalments).

Flat rate scheme

- Optional scheme for business with tax exclusive taxable turnover up to £150,000.
- Must leave if VAT inclusive taxable supplies exceed £230,000.
- Flat rate of VAT applies to total tax inclusive turnover.
- Normal VAT invoice issued to VAT registered customers.
- The flat rate percentage to use will be given to you in your exam.

Notes

Notes

Notes

Notes

Notes

Notes

Notes